Quotes, Questions & Actions
for Global Understanding

Also by Jan Gault

BOOKS
The Mighty Power of Your Beliefs…
Dream, Believe, Prosper
Free Time—Making Your Leisure Count

AUDIO/CD PROGRAMS
Inspirational/Motivational Podcasts
Perseverance & Passion; Strategies for Success
25 Ways to Build Self-Esteem & Success
The Principle of Purpose
Vision & Courage
Prosperity Principles & Beliefs

PERSONAL-GLOBAL EMPOWERMENT &
PROSPERITY SERIES
Explorations & Activities
7 Steps to Personal-Global Empowerment
Personal-Global Empowerment Calendar
Inspiration Booklets
Choices for a Better Life, Community & World

Bulk Purchase Discounts
Books are available at quantity discounts with bulk purchase
for business, educational, or sales promotional use. For
information, please telephone/fax: 800-851-6114

**For information on scheduling Jan to speak at your next
event, or on ordering books, CDs and other products by
Jan, please Email info@drjan.net or visit her web site:
www.drjan.net/betterworld**

Quotes, Questions & Actions for Global Understanding

Book One

Jan L. Gault, Ph.D.

Ocean Manor

Cover Design by Leo Gonzalez

Images provided by Dreamstime.com

Copyright© 2006 by Jan L. Gault

Library of Congress Cataloging-in-Publication Data
Gault, Jan L.
Quotes, Questions & Actions for Global Understanding
/ Jan L. Gault—1st ed.
p. cm.
1. Inspiration   2. Social change   3. Gift book   I. Title.

Library of Congress Control Number: 2006924897

ISBN-13: 978-0-923699-27-7 (pbk.)
ISBN-10: 0-923699-27-9 (pbk.)

Printed in the United States of America

10 9 8 7 6 5 4 3 2 1

This book is printed on acid-free paper.

This book is dedicated to each of you acting to create a kinder,
more compassionate, cooperative and just world.

I also dedicate it to all the wonderful people working to make
a difference within my
Favorite Organizations

**Action Without Borders, Amnesty International, Audubon
Society, Better World Club, Books for a Better World,
Center for Global Nonviolence, Childreach, Common
Cause, Doctors Without Borders, Educators for Social
Responsibility, Feminist Majority Foundation, M. K.
Gandhi Institute, Global Citizens Network, Global
Exchange, Global Heroes, Habitat for Humanity, Heifer
Project International, Human Rights Education Associates,
Human Rights Watch, IFUW, Institute of Noetic Sciences,
Interfaith Alliance, Katalysis, Nature Conservatory, Oxfam
International, PETA, Psychologists for Social
Responsibility, Red Hat Society, Seva Foundation, Sierra
Club, Society for the Psychological Study of Social Issues,
Soroptimist International, Southern Poverty Law Center,
White Ribbon Campaign, Worldwatch Institute, Women
for Women International, Working Assets**

Contents

Introduction

Each of us sees the world through the eyes of the particular culture into which we were born and raised. What seems natural to us is dictated by all the facets of the culture we've become familiar with—its customs, laws, mores, education, social, political and economic systems, forms of entertainment, and artifacts.

To fully understand others—whether they live next door or halfway across the world, we must go beyond knowledge. True understanding springs from the depths of being, and paradoxically transcends knowledge. When we learn *why* a person thinks, feels, believes and acts as they do, we are on the path to understanding them. Only when we are able to see the world through their eyes rather than our own particular culture of customs and habits, will we be in a position to leave judgment behind to communicate openly and intelligently. Only then can we peacefully and effectively resolve conflicts.

A deeper understanding of others around the globe will form the basis for a reduction of suspicion, distrust and hostility among those who differ from us. A wiser understanding will help promote compassion, kindness and hopefully prompt action toward the resolution of difficult problems such as poverty, suffering and violence.

Understanding and acceptance of others differences is a first step toward generating communication and positive change. It does not imply condonance, only nonjudgment and a lack of condemnation. For those cultural practices which we deem unjust or inhumane, our role is to educate and influence through peaceful means.

The goals of this short work are to increase understanding through the combined methods of inspiration, critical questioning and action prompts. These can be used by the individual alone or within a group discussion setting. Questions are a powerful catalyst for creating change. When we ask ourselves the tough questions, our minds and hearts move to respond. Our energy becomes focused on finding a solution. Provocative questions both focus and direct our energy toward answers and alternatives. Using this tool can help to reduce apathy and encourage individual responsibility in solving tough global problems.

I sincerely hope that this little book will stimulate your thinking, expand your awareness and influence you to take positive steps toward a richer global understanding.

Warm Aloha,
Jan L. Gault
Kailua, Hawaii
May 2006

Suggestions for Reading

I recommend that you target one to three actions each week to make a part of your regular routine. Use the inspirational messages and sample actions on each page as triggers for your own imagination and insights. Refer to the list of seventy-five specific actions at the end of the book for additional ideas.

Memorize and post those inspirations that are closest to your heart. Make them a part of your consciousness, thinking and living. Know that whatever efforts you make in the service of humanity matters. Our world is improving each day, each week and each year because of people like you—individuals who care enough to read a book such as this and who are seeking a greater understanding and a kinder, more compassionate world.

Week One
A Richer Understanding

Total Listening Brings Understanding

"When we talk about understanding, surely it takes place only when the mind listens completely—the mind being your heart, your nerves, your ears—when you give your whole attention to it."

–Jiddu Krishnamurti

Questions to Consider:
1. Where would you place your level of understanding about yourself, other cultures and world issues? Are you able to fully listen when presented with worldviews that do not align with your own?
2. Are you taking steps regularly to enhance your understanding? In what ways?

My Choice & Commitment:
I choose to   (Circle One)
  A. Do nothing about this now.
  B. Consider this further.
  C. Take Action.

Specific Action Steps I Will Take:
(**Sample Action:** I will make contact with one person who has different beliefs than me, ask questions, and open my mind and heart to listen to them completely without judgment.)

1._____
2._____
3._____

When? (Circle One)
    Today   This Week   This Month   Other_____

Understanding Rather Than Destruction

"Our understanding of how to live with one another is still far behind our knowledge of how to destroy one another."

–Lyndon B. Johnson

Questions to Consider:
1. How can you and your enemies increase your understanding of how to live more harmoniously with one another?
2. What steps can you take to live more peacefully with those in your life?

My Choice & Commitment:
I choose to   (Circle One)
A. Do nothing about this now.
B. Consider this further.
C. Take Action.

Specific Action Steps I Will Take:
(**Sample Action:** I will begin taking individual responsibility for peace by practicing peaceful means of conflict resolution in my home environment.)

1._____
2._____
3._____

When? (Circle One)
Today   This Week   This Month   Other_____

Spiral Growth of Understanding

*"The growth of understanding follows an ascending spiral
rather than a straight line."*

–Joanna Field

Questions to Consider:
1. Do you get discouraged when the world seems to take a step backward in understanding?
2. Can you visualize the movement of understanding in the consciousness of humankind as an ascending spiral, much like our genetic codes? Do you see how this perspective might be helpful when confronted with setbacks?

My Choice & Commitment:
I choose to   (Circle One)
    A. Do nothing about this now.
    B. Consider this further.
    C. Take Action.

Specific Action Steps I Will Take:
(**Sample Action:** I will make a list of seven ways in which the growth of understanding is improving in the world to keep before me when I become discouraged and disillusioned about humanity's errors.)

1._____
2._____
3._____

When? (Circle One)
    Today   This Week   This Month   Other_____

For Full Understanding We Need to Go Beyond the Intellect

"We should not pretend to understand the world only by the intellect. The judgment of the intellect is only part of the truth."

–Carl Jung

Questions to Consider:
1. Do you tend to rely solely on your own experiential base of reasoning, perceptions and interpretations to understand the world?
2. Can you open your mind to the possibility that a more comprehensive understanding of the world requires sometimes going beyond your intellect?

My Choice & Commitment:
I choose to   (Circle One)
- A. Do nothing about this now.
- B. Consider this further.
- C. Take Action.

Specific Action Steps I Will Take:
(**Sample Action:** I will set aside a time to revisit my internal reality and look beyond my intellect at impressions, images, space and silence to explore new ways of seeing things and maximizing my understanding.)

1._____
2._____
3._____

When? (Circle One)
Today   This Week   This Month   Other_____

An Eye for an Eye Negates Amity

"It is time to realize that violence with violence and hatred with hatred will not foster amity and understanding."

–Swami Nirmalanda

Questions to Consider:
1. If you have realized this important truth, what is your role in educating others here?
2. If you allow this eye-for-an-eye doctrine to exist when you could speak out against it, what does that say about you?

My Choice & Commitment:
I choose to   (Circle One)
    A. Do nothing about this now.
    B. Consider this further.
    C. Take Action.

Specific Action Steps I Will Take:
(**Sample Action:** I will draft a well-thought out letter on this issue and Email it to twenty online newspapers. I will encourage my friends and family to do likewise.)

1._____
2._____
3._____

When? (Circle One)
    Today   This Week   This Month   Other_____

Need for Action Guided by Understanding

"Understanding, and action proceeding from understanding and guided by it, is one weapon against the world's bombardment, the one medicine, the one instrument by which liberty, health, and joy may be shaped...in the individual, and in the race."

–James Agee

Questions to Consider:
1. Are your actions guided by understanding?
2. Do you believe that your community and nation's actions are based on understanding? In what ways can you contribute to the gap between understanding and action?

My Choice & Commitment:
I choose to   (Circle One)
   A. Do nothing about this now.
   B. Consider this further.
   C. Take Action.

Specific Action Steps I Will Take:
(**Sample Action:** I will take one insight I have learned and translate it into a specific action that will positively impact another person's life.)

1._____
2._____
3._____

When? (Circle One)
   Today   This Week   This Month   Other_____

Understanding Makes Us Free

"The highest activity a human being can attain is learning for understanding, because to understand is to be free."

–Baruch (Benedict de) Spinoza

Questions to Consider:
1. In what ways does learning for understanding make us free?
2. Is there an area in your life where you can increase your understanding?

My Choice & Commitment:
I choose to   (Circle One)
   A. Do nothing about this now.
   B. Consider this further.
   C. Take Action.

Specific Action Steps I Will Take:
(**Sample Action:** I will send a picture to a child in a third world country expressing what freedom means to me. I will include a notebook and crayons for them to respond.)

1._____
2._____
3._____

When? (Circle One)
   Today   This Week   This Month   Other_____

Week Two
An Expanded Global Perspective
Harmonious Living

Global Harmony Begins in Individual Minds

"First there must be order and harmony within your own mind."

–Confucius

Questions to Consider:
1. What can you do to resolve any disruptive conflicts in your mind?
2. Have you learned to let go of debilitating frustration and anger when it compromises your life?

My Choice & Commitment:
I choose to   (Circle One)
   A. Do nothing about this now.
   B. Consider this further.
   C. Take Action.

Specific Action Steps I Will Take:
(**Sample Action:** I will read an article on resolving internal conflicts, and practice what I have learned by role playing with a friend.)

1._____
2._____
3._____

When? (Circle One)
   Today   This Week   This Month   Other_____

Limited View of the World

"No man ever looks at the world with pristine eyes. He sees it edited by a definite set of customs and institutions and ways of thinking."

–Ruth Fulton Benedict

Questions to Consider:
1. How have your family, education and country's customs influenced your ways of thinking about the world?
2. Have you ever tried to step outside of your culture's beliefs and practices and see them through the eyes of other cultures?

My Choice & Commitment:
I choose to   (Circle One)
   A. Do nothing about this now.
   B. Consider this further.
   C. Take Action.

Specific Action Steps I Will Take:
(**Sample Action:** I will spend fifteen minutes looking at my culture through the eyes of another culture. E.g., if you live in America, look at your culture from the perspective of someone living in Egypt.)

1._____
2._____
3._____

When? (Circle One)
   Today   This Week   This Month   Other_____

Do You Share the Crime of Oppression?

"He who allows oppression shares the crime."

–Erasmus

Questions to Consider:
1. Are you allowing oppression to exist in your community, nation or the world?
2. Is there one small action you can take to help put an end to that oppression? What?

My Choice & Commitment:
I choose to   (Circle One)
A. Do nothing about this now.
B. Consider this further.
C. Take Action.

Specific Action Steps I Will Take:
(**Sample Action:** I will speak out against oppression whenever and wherever I find it. I will begin in my own neighborhood.)

1._____
2._____
3._____

When? (Circle One)
    Today   This Week   This Month   Other_____

A World Community

"A world community can exist only with world communication, which means something more than extensive shortwave facilities scattered about the globe. It means common understanding, a common tradition, common ideas, and common ideals."

–Robert M. Hutchins

Questions to Consider:
1. What are some of the common understandings, traditions, ideas, and ideals of your nation that are shared with others?
2. Is it possible to increase these among us and improve world communication? How?

My Choice & Commitment:
I choose to   (Circle One)
    A. Do nothing about this now.
    B. Consider this further.
    C. Take Action.

Specific Action Steps I Will Take:
(**Sample Action:** I will initiate a new correspondence with a person in another country and explore common ideas and ideals.)

1._____
2._____
3._____

When? (Circle One)
    Today   This Week   This Month   Other_____

World Problems Will Be Solved by New Visions

"The problems of the world cannot possibly be solved by skeptics or cynics whose horizons are limited by the obvious realities. We need men (and women) who can dream of things that never were."

–John F. Kennedy

Questions to Consider:
1. Are you allowing skeptics and cynics to influence your thinking?
2. Can you create a new vision for solving a problem in the world? Why not?

My Choice & Commitment:
I choose to   (Circle One)
- A. Do nothing about this now.
- B. Consider this further.
- C. Take Action.

Specific Action Steps I Will Take:
(**Sample Action:** I will meet with like-minded people and together we will invent new visions for solving difficult world problems.)

1._____
2._____
3._____

When? (Circle One)
    Today   This Week   This Month   Other_____

We See the World as We Are

"We do not see things as they are, we see them as we are."

–The Talmud

Questions to Consider:
1. How does your background of family, social conditioning and experiences color your perceptions of the world and global issues?
2. Can you identify any prejudices you have here?

My Choice & Commitment:
I choose to   (Circle One)
- A. Do nothing about this now.
- B. Consider this further.
- C. Take Action.

Specific Action Steps I Will Take:
(**Sample Action:** I will write a two paragraph description of one significant experience I've had in my life and how it has affected my worldview.)

1._____
2._____
3._____

When? (Circle One)
    Today   This Week   This Month   Other_____

Unity of All

"Only the unity of all can bring the well-being of all."

–Robert Muller

Questions to Consider:
1. What are some of the ways that you can reach out to bridge the gap among other nations?
2. Is there one action you can take to open up positive communication with a person in another nation?

My Choice & Commitment:
I choose to   (Circle One)
  A. Do nothing about this now.
  B. Consider this further.
  C. Take Action.

Specific Action Steps I Will Take:
(**Sample Action:** I will identify a person in another nation with a similar interest through an online forum and correspond with them by Email.)

1._____
2._____
3._____

When? (Circle One)
  Today   This Week   This Month   Other_____

Week Three
Education for an
Interdependent World

Educate the Heart Not Just the Mind

"Educating the mind without educating the heart is no education at all."

–Aristotle

Questions to Consider:
1. Are the teachers in your community teaching the heart principles of love, kindness and compassion?
2. What is your role in this process?

My Choice & Commitment:
I choose to   (Circle One)
A. Do nothing about this now.
B. Consider this further.
C. Take Action.

Specific Action Steps I Will Take:
(**Sample Action:** I will speak with teachers in my community about how we might better make "educating the heart" part of the class curriculum.)

1._____
2._____
3._____

When? (Circle One)
    Today   This Week   This Month   Other_____

Education or Catastrophe?

"Human history becomes more and more a race between education and catastrophe."

–H. G. Wells

Questions to Consider:
1. What steps can individuals and society take to insure an education of understanding for the future?
2. How can we best impact global movements for an education that includes the values of compassion, human rights, and conflict resolution through nonviolent means?

My Choice & Commitment:
I choose to   (Circle One)
  A. Do nothing about this now.
  B. Consider this further.
  C. Take Action.

Specific Action Steps I Will Take:
(**Sample Action:** I will identify and follow through with one means for educating myself and one other person on the value of conflict resolution through nonviolent means.)

1._____
2._____
3._____

When? (Circle One)
  Today   This Week   This Month   Other_____

On School Curriculum

"My dream is that there will be a day when, in our schools, we will teach the history of the prophet and less of the history of the generals and their instruments of war."

–Rev. Jose "Chencho" Alas

Questions to Consider:
1. Do you think that if the teaching in our schools incorporated the principles of love, compassion and kindness as taught by the prophets, our children would be less prone to violence and prejudice?
2. Whose responsibility is it to suggest to our teachers and educators that we include this as part of the school curriculum?

My Choice & Commitment:
I choose to   (Circle One)
   A. Do nothing about this now.
   B. Consider this further.
   C. Take Action.

Specific Action Steps I Will Take:
(Sample Action: I will visit one high school in my community and talk with a social studies teacher about the possibility of incorporating the positive principles taught by the prophets in their history lessons.)

1._____
2._____
3._____

When? (Circle One)
   Today   This Week   This Month   Other_____

A Culture of Nonviolence

"Young people must learn at home and in school that violence may not be a means of settling differences with others. Only thus can a culture of nonviolence be created."

–Dr. Hans Kung

Questions to Consider:
1. Are the children whose life you touch learning that violence is not a means of settling differences with others?
2. What are some of the alternatives to violence for settling differences we can give our children?

My Choice & Commitment:
I choose to   (Circle One)
   A. Do nothing about this now.
   B. Consider this further.
   C. Take Action.

Specific Action Steps I Will Take:
(**Sample Action:** I will refrain from using corporeal punishment with my own children and teach them alternatives to violence for settling differences.)

1._____
2._____
3._____

When? (Circle One)
   Today   This Week   This Month   Other_____

Fate of Empires

"All who have meditated on the art of governing mankind have been convinced that the fate of empires depends on the education of youth."

–Aristotle

Questions to Consider:
1. What education are the youth of the world receiving from the mass media, schools, video games and other sources?
2. Is it an education that will move the world in the direction of peace and prosperity, compassion and understanding?

My Choice & Commitment:
I choose to   (Circle One)
   A. Do nothing about this now.
   B. Consider this further.
   C. Take Action.

Specific Action Steps I Will Take:
(**Sample Action:** I will do my share in the education of youth by arranging to give a talk at a community college in my area on the importance of global understanding.)

1._____
2._____
3._____

When? (Circle One)
   Today   This Week   This Month   Other_____

Ignorance in Action

"Nothing is more terrifying than ignorance in action."

–Goethe

Questions to Consider:
1. How can we guard against serious blunders in our quest to understand and resolve global issues?
2. What greater role could our schools and the media play to minimize costly "ignorance in action"?

My Choice & Commitment:
I choose to   (Circle One)
   A. Do nothing about this now.
   B. Consider this further.
   C. Take Action.

Specific Action Steps I Will Take:
(**Sample Action:** I will support an online global media group who is disseminating diverse points of view from members of countries throughout the world and whose leadership has a reputation for honesty and integrity. My support will take the form of financial aid or volunteering my time according to my talents, skills and expertise.)

1._____
2._____
3._____

When? (Circle One)
   Today   This Week   This Month   Other_____

Don't Lose Faith in Humanity

"You must not lose faith in humanity. Humanity is an ocean—if a few drops of the ocean are dirty, the ocean is not dirty."

–Mohandas K. Gandhi

Questions to Consider:
1. Has media coverage of violence and inhumane acts by men and women disillusioned you about the overall goodness of humanity?
2. Did you know that all behavior is learned and no one is born bad? Can you entertain the idea that if someone has grown up in a dysfunctional home or culture and been taught nothing but hatred and violence from an early age, they will likely exhibit these same behaviors? Is it not a wonderful revelation that we are not born bad, and that all undesirable learned behavior can be unlearned with the proper education and practice?

My Choice & Commitment:
I choose to   (Circle One)
- A. Do nothing about this now.
- B. Consider this further.
- C. Take Action.

Specific Action Steps I Will Take:
(**Sample Action:** Instead of exposing myself to all the bad news in the media from newspapers, television and the web, I will take time to focus on the many good things people are doing for humanity.)

1._____
2._____
3._____

When? (Circle One)
　　　Today　　This Week　　This Month　　Other_____

Week Four
Cultivating a World Conscience
Sharing the Responsibility

World without Conscience?

"The world has achieved brilliance without conscience. Ours is a world of nuclear giants and ethical infants."

–Omar N. Bradley

Questions to Consider:
1. Has humanity's conscience of attending to the needs of the less fortunate plummeted into apathy?
2. What actions can you and others take to help awaken our moral conscience?

My Choice & Commitment:
I choose to   (Circle One)
A. Do nothing about this now.
B. Consider this further.
C. Take Action.

Specific Action Steps I Will Take:
(**Sample Action:** I will awaken my global conscience by listening to a world ethics lecture online.)

1._____
2._____
3._____

When? (Circle One)
Today   This Week   This Month   Other_____

You Only Need to Do Your Part

"Let everyone sweep in front of his own door, and the whole world will be clean."

–Johann Wolfgang von Goethe

Questions to Consider:
1. Why are there so few who assume this responsibility for themselves?
2. Where might you begin in meeting this responsibility?

My Choice & Commitment:
I choose to   (Circle One)
   A. Do nothing about this now.
   B. Consider this further.
   C. Take Action.

Specific Action Steps I Will Take:
(**Sample Action:**   I will take one weekend to release all negativity and replenish my mind and soul by listening to the sounds of beautiful music, enjoying a sunset and anonymously giving a gift to someone in need.)

1._____
2._____
3._____

When? (Circle One)
   Today   This Week   This Month   Other_____

Keep Your Heart Open to Those less Fortunate

"Let us touch the dying, the poor, the lonely and the unwanted according to the graces we have received and let us not be ashamed or slow to do the humble work."

–Mother Teresa

Questions to Consider:
1. Growing up in a culture where material values are dominant, it is easy to forget the pain and suffering of those who are less fortunate. Is there someone whose life you can ease by a word of comfort or a simple act of kindness?
2. Are you ashamed of letting yourself be defined by humble work? Why?

My Choice & Commitment:
I choose to   (Circle One)
   A. Do nothing about this now.
   B. Consider this further.
   C. Take Action.

Specific Action Steps I Will Take:
(**Sample Action:** I will send a card with a personal note to someone in distress.)

1._____
2._____
3._____

When? (Circle One)
   Today   This Week   This Month   Other_____

Responsibility Lies within You

"You must take personal responsibility. You cannot change the circumstances, the seasons, or the wind, but you can change yourself. That is something you have charge of."

–Jim Rohn

Questions to Consider:
1. Did you know that you have an enormous power? The power to change yourself?
2. What motivation do you have to change yourself? Can you see the link between changing yourself and changing the world? If you could change one tiny aspect of your personality or behavior, what would it be? Why?

My Choice & Commitment:
I choose to   (Circle One)
   A. Do nothing about this now.
   B. Consider this further.
   C. Take Action.

Specific Action Steps I Will Take:
(**Sample Action:** I will motivate myself by reading stories of those who have dramatically changed their lives and the lives of others by changing themselves.)

1._____
2._____
3._____

When? (Circle One)
   Today   This Week   This Month   Other_____

A Call to Share the Responsibility for World Misery

"Whoever is spared personal pain must feel himself called to help in diminishing the pain of others. We must all carry our share of the misery which lies upon the world."

–Albert Schweitzer

Questions to Consider:
1. Are you one of the lucky ones who has clean water to drink, food to eat and a shelter to protect you from the rain, snow and hot sun?
2. What small step can you take to share the responsibility toward the demise of world misery?

My Choice & Commitment:
I choose to   (Circle One)
- A. Do nothing about this now.
- B. Consider this further.
- C. Take Action.

Specific Action Steps I Will Take:
(**Sample Action:** I will put all the coins I receive as change into a fund to help a war disaster victim in another country.)

1._____
2._____
3._____

When? (Circle One)
   Today   This Week   This Month   Other_____

Apathy

"Science may have found a cure for most evils; but it has found no remedy for the worst of them all—the apathy of human beings."

–Helen Keller

Questions to Consider:
1. Why do we sometimes get so caught up in our own activities and problems that we close our minds to the injustices and suffering of the vast majority of people in the world?
2. What are some steps we can take to guard against this apathy?

My Choice & Commitment:
I choose to   (Circle One)
A. Do nothing about this now.
B. Consider this further.
C. Take Action.

Specific Action Steps I Will Take:
(**Sample Action:** I will block out one hour to consider actions I can consistently take to guard against my own apathy and to influence others in the same direction.)

1._____
2._____
3._____

When? (Circle One)
   Today   This Week   This Month   Other_____

Share the Toil & Lighten the Load

"Light is the task when many share the toil."

–Homer

Questions to Consider:
1. Are you sharing the toil of ending poverty, suffering and pain?
2. Can you think of one way to carry your share that would be both satisfying and fun?

My Choice & Commitment:
I choose to   (Circle One)
A. Do nothing about this now.
B. Consider this further.
C. Take Action.

Specific Action Steps I Will Take:
(**Sample Action:** To bring home the axiom that "my best contribution to others will derive from a labor of love", I will take one passion that I have and explore how I can use it to ease the pain and suffering of a person in a "foreign" country.)

1._____
2._____
3._____

When? (Circle One)
Today   This Week   This Month   Other_____

Week Five
Service to Others
Kindness & Compassion

Greatness Determined by Service

"Everyone has the power for greatness, not for fame but for greatness, because greatness is determined by service."

--Martin Luther King, Jr.

Questions to Consider:
1. Have you realized your greatness in service to others?
2. How might you more fully tap into your greatness?

My Choice & Commitment:
I choose to   (Circle One)
A. Do nothing about this now.
B. Consider this further.
C. Take Action.

Specific Action Steps I Will Take:
(**Sample Action:** I will spend thirty minutes reflecting on how I might better live up to my potential for greatness.)

1._____
2._____
3._____

When? (Circle One)
    Today   This Week   This Month   Other_____

Acts of Kindness Create a Better World

"Constant kindness can accomplish much. As the sun makes ice melt, kindness causes misunderstanding, mistrust, and hostility to evaporate."

–Albert Schweitzer

Questions to Consider:
1. Has someone's act of kindness made a difference in your life?
2. Have you made acts of kindness to others a regular part of your life?

My Choice & Commitment:
I choose to   (Circle One)
   A. Do nothing about this now.
   B. Consider this further.
   C. Take Action.

Specific Action Steps I Will Take:
(**Sample Action**: I will perform one act of kindness to begin making kindness a regular part of my life.)

1._____
2._____
3._____

When? (Circle One)
Today   This Week   This Month   Other_____

Widen the Circle of Compassion

"Our task must be to free ourselves from this prison by widening our circle of compassion to embrace all living beings and all of nature."

–Albert Einstein

Questions to Consider:
1. Does your circle of compassion extend beyond your immediate family and friends?
2. Can you embrace the brotherhood and sisterhood of all living beings and nature?

My Choice & Commitment:
I choose to   (Circle One)
A. Do nothing about this now.
B. Consider this further.
C. Take Action.

Specific Action Steps I Will Take:
(**Sample Action:** I will set aside fifteen minutes to meditate on ways to widen my circle of compassion to all living beings and nature.)

1._____
2._____
3._____

When? (Circle One)
Today   This Week   This Month   Other_____

Talents to Help Society's Less Fortunate

"...Each of us is a trustee of the talents we possess and, instead of exploiting these talents for selfish gains, we should use some of the talent to help the less fortunate in society. We must serve humanity with compassion, not pity."

–Arun Gandhi

Questions to Consider:
1. Are some of your talents being used to help the less fortunate in society?
2. What are some ways we can more compassionately serve humanity?

My Choice & Commitment:
I choose to   (Circle One)
- A. Do nothing about this now.
- B. Consider this further.
- C. Take Action.

Specific Action Steps I Will Take:
(**Sample Action:** I will take stock of my talents and identify one strength that I can employ to better serve humanity.)

1._____
2._____
3._____

When? (Circle One)
   Today   This Week   This Month   Other_____

Become Part of the Solution

"Our job this day is to become part of the answer to the world's immense and protracted suffering rather than continuing our ancient task of becoming part of the difficulty."

–Hugh Prather

Questions to Consider:
1. What role are you, your community and your nation playing in the great task of alleviating world suffering?
2. When you focus on other people's plight rather than your own, how does it affect you? How does it make you feel?

My Choice & Commitment:
I choose to   (Circle One)
   A. Do nothing about this now.
   B. Consider this further.
   C. Take Action.

Specific Action Steps I Will Take:
(**Sample Action:** I will do my part by focusing on the needs of the world's millions who do not have clean water to drink, food to eat or shelters from harsh weather. Instead of feeling helpless I will take one small step toward alleviating their distress by making a donation or doing volunteer work.)

1._____
2._____
3._____

When? (Circle One)
   Today   This Week   This Month   Other_____

Zero Tolerance for Inhumane Acts

"We should have zero tolerance for those who intentionally inflict pain on another, whether they live next door or thousands of miles away."

–Juanita Vance

Questions to Consider:
1. Are you aware of laws, customs or practices that intentionally violate a person's rights to humane treatment?
2. What steps can you, your family, organization or corporation take to initiate positive change here?

My Choice & Commitment:
I choose to   (Circle One)
   A. Do nothing about this now.
   B. Consider this further.
   C. Take Action.

Specific Action Steps I Will Take:
(**Sample Action:** I will send a letter to the editor of my newspaper on a practice that violates a person's right to humane treatment.)

1._____
2._____
3._____

When? (Circle One)
   Today   This Week   This Month   Other_____

The Purpose of Human Life

"The purpose of human life is to serve, and to show compassion and the will to help others."

–Albert Schweitzer

Questions to Consider:
1. How does this translate into your life? Is a portion of your time spent in community service for those in need?
2. What else might you do to help those who are less fortunate?

My Choice & Commitment:
I choose to   (Circle One)
A. Do nothing about this now.
B. Consider this further.
C. Take Action.

Specific Action Steps I Will Take:
(**Sample Action:** I will volunteer to chair a cultural understanding group in one of my community service organizations.)

1._____
2._____
3._____

When? (Circle One)
     Today   This Week   This Month   Other_____

Week Six
Improving the World Through Better Thinking & Beliefs

Believe in Life

"To believe in immortality is one thing, but it is first needful to believe in life."

–Robert Louis Stevenson

Questions to Consider:
1. Do you believe in the miracle of life? Do you see life as a blessing—packed with new adventures and opportunities?
2. What are your beliefs about life? How are these beliefs affecting you and the rest of the world?

My Choice & Commitment:
I choose to   (Circle One)
- A. Do nothing about this now.
- B. Consider this further.
- C. Take Action.

Specific Action Steps I Will Take:
(**Sample Action:** Complete the sentence: "Life is …" five times. Next, note how these beliefs are played out in your life.)

1._____
2._____
3._____

When? (Circle One)
   Today   This Week   This Month   Other_____

Rise Up to a New Level of Thinking

"The significant problems we face cannot be solved at the same level of thinking we were at when we created them."

–Albert Einstein

Questions to Consider:
1. Did you know psychologists have identified a level of thinking called metacognition: "the awareness of your own cognitive processes and the ability to monitor and control those processes"?
2. How can we encourage people to explore new ways of thinking and shifts in consciousness to gain greater insights and solutions to modern day dilemmas?

My Choice & Commitment:
I choose to   (Circle One)
- A. Do nothing about this now.
- B. Consider this further.
- C. Take Action.

Specific Action Steps I Will Take:
(**Sample Action:** I will read an article on "Improving Your Creative Thinking Abilities" to facilitate my mind's expansion.)

1._____
2._____
3._____

When? (Circle One)
   Today   This Week   This Month   Other_____

Big Issues

"Just because a problem is widespread, seemingly irresolvable and has no easy answers is no reason not to address it—all the more reason to put our minds together, both individually and globally."

–Juanita Vance

Questions to Consider:
1. Do the problems of world poverty, suffering, and violence seem insurmountable?
2. Did you know that the first step in solving a problem (whether personal or global and regardless of its magnitude) is a belief that it's possible?

My Choice & Commitment:
I choose to   (Circle One)
   A. Do nothing about this now.
   B. Consider this further.
   C. Take Action.

Specific Action Steps I Will Take:
(**Sample Action:** I will take one world problem that appears insurmountable, and bolster my belief in a viable solution to it by imagining ten strategies that "could" work.)

1._____
2._____
3._____

When? (Circle One)
   Today   This Week   This Month   Other_____

Your Habitual Thoughts Will Determine Your Legacy to the World

"What you hold in your thoughts is what you bring into the world."

–High Star

Questions to Consider:
1. What kinds of thoughts regularly inhabit your mind?
2. Have you ever considered that the energy contained in your habitual thoughts will be what you manifest in the world? What thoughts are you holding on to?

My Choice & Commitment:
I choose to   (Circle One)
A. Do nothing about this now.
B. Consider this further.
C. Take Action.

Specific Action Steps I Will Take:
(**Sample Action:** I will keep a "thought log" for eight hours to evaluate the thought energy I am bringing into the world.)

1._____
2._____
3._____

When? (Circle One)
Today   This Week   This Month   Other_____

Change Your Beliefs to Change the World

"The most powerful thing you can do to change the world is to change your own beliefs about the nature of life, people, and reality to something more positive...and begin to act accordingly."

–Shakti Gawain

Questions to Consider:
1. What are your beliefs about the nature of life, people and reality? Do you see life as an adventure or as a struggle and something to get through? Do you generally trust others or view them with suspicion and distrust?
2. Can you see how your beliefs trigger actions and that making changes here can have positive outcomes in your life and the life of others?

My Choice & Commitment:
I choose to   (Circle One)
   A. Do nothing about this now.
   B. Consider this further.
   C. Take Action.

Specific Action Steps I Will Take:
(**Sample Action:** List five beliefs that you have about people. Take one of these that is negatively impacting your relationships with others and replace it with an opposite, more positive belief. Practice "acting as if" you owned that belief.)

1._____
2._____
3._____

When? (Circle One)
   Today   This Week   This Month   Other_____

Believe in a Solution

"Believe it can be done. When you believe something can be done, really believe, your mind will find the ways to do it. Believing a solution paves the way to solution."

–David J. Schwartz

Questions to Consider:
1. Has doubt kept you from arriving at a solution to a problem you face?
2. If you cannot yet fully believe that a solution will be found, can you open your mind to the possibility? And then begin anew?

My Choice & Commitment:
I choose to   (Circle One)
A. Do nothing about this now.
B. Consider this further.
C. Take Action.

Specific Action Steps I Will Take:
(**Sample Action:** I will strengthen my belief in my ability to arrive at a solution by writing down five reasons why I'm capable of solving a problem I face.)

1._____
2._____
3._____

When? (Circle One)
Today   This Week   This Month   Other_____

Consequences of Not Thinking

"What luck for the rulers that men do not think."

–Adolph Hitler

Questions to Consider:
1. Why do the majority of us run on automatic pilot most of the time? How can we break out of this nonthinking posture—particularly when life and death, human suffering and injustices are at stake?
2. What are some of the obvious consequences for both you and humanity of not thinking through our choices and actions?

My Choice & Commitment:
I choose to   (Circle One)
   A. Do nothing about this now.
   B. Consider this further.
   C. Take Action.

Specific Action Steps I Will Take:
(**Sample Action:** I will write down five unwanted consequences I have had as a result of not thinking; and five unwanted outcomes the world has had as a result of many people not thinking.)

1._____
2._____
3._____

When? (Circle One)
   Today   This Week   This Month   Other_____

Week Seven
Empowered Change

Change

"They say time changes things, but you actually have to change them yourself."

–Andy Warhol

Questions to Consider:
1. Have you hoped that a situation or the world would get better with the passage of time?
2. Can you think of one contribution that you might make to improve the world in which you live?

My Choice & Commitment:
I choose to   (Circle One)
A. Do nothing about this now.
B. Consider this further.
C. Take Action.

Specific Action Steps I Will Take:
(**Sample Action:** I will identify one talent or skill I can develop more fully to use in the service of humanity.)

1._____
2._____
3._____

When? (Circle One)
    Today   This Week   This Month   Other_____

World Progress Depends on the Unreasonable Man

"The reasonable man adapts himself to the world; the unreasonable one persists in trying to adapt the world to himself. Therefore all progress depends on the unreasonable man."

–George Bernard Shaw

Questions to Consider:
1. Does this idea make sense to you? In what ways?
2. Are you adapting yourself to the world even when you believe it to be out of sync with your heart and sense of justice?

My Choice & Commitment:
I choose to   (Circle One)
    A. Do nothing about this now.
    B. Consider this further.
    C. Take Action.

Specific Action Steps I Will Take:
(**Sample Action:** I will refuse to be "reasonable" when called upon to adapt to popular consensus when it goes against my heartfelt values or better judgment.)

1._____
2._____
3._____

When? (Circle One)
    Today   This Week   This Month   Other_____

Changing Times

"We must adjust to changing times and still hold to unchanging principles."

–Jimmy Carter

Questions to Consider:
1. Do you think that humanitarian principles have fallen by the wayside under the stress of changing times?
2. Is there some small action you can take that will contribute to a more humane, compassionate world?

My Choice & Commitment:
I choose to   (Circle One)
- A. Do nothing about this now.
- B. Consider this further.
- C. Take Action.

Specific Action Steps I Will Take:
(**Sample Action:** I will support a community group that adheres to the unchanging principles of love, kindness and goodwill.)

1._____
2._____
3._____

When? (Circle One)
Today   This Week   This Month   Other_____

Condemnation Oppresses

"We cannot change anything until we accept it. Condemnation does not liberate, it oppresses."

–C. G. Jung

Questions to Consider:
1. Since acceptance (not condonance) of a situation is primary for change to occur, how might we shift our position here when facing unwanted conditions?
2. Can we learn to refrain from judging and condemning those situations and people who differ from us? How?

My Choice & Commitment:
I choose to   (Circle One)
- A. Do nothing about this now.
- B. Consider this further.
- C. Take Action.

Specific Action Steps I Will Take:
(**Sample Action:** Take a sheet of paper and write down six ways in which you have judged or condemned people in another country. Visualize the world of all people as one giant human of which you are a part. Or viewed another way, visualize yourself as one giant human of which everyone else is a part. Would you chop off your hand?)

1._____
2._____
3._____

When? (Circle One)
    Today   This Week   This Month   Other_____

The Chief Obstacle to Progress of the Human Race

"The chief obstacle to the progress of the human race is the human race."

–Don Marquis

Questions to Consider:
1. How would you define "progress of the human race"? Peaceful coexistence with other nations? An end to world poverty, suffering and pain? Spiritual fulfillment?
2. Do you think a new species must evolve before progress defined in these terms can come about? Is that possible?

My Choice & Commitment:
I choose to   (Circle One)
A. Do nothing about this now.
B. Consider this further.
C. Take Action.

Specific Action Steps I Will Take:
(**Sample Action:** List five changes that you believe must occur before we can have significant progress of the human race.)

1._____
2._____
3._____

When? (Circle One)
Today   This Week   This Month   Other_____

79

Focus on the Good

"Every year of my life I grow more convinced that it is wisest and best to fix our attention on the beautiful and the good, and dwell as little as possible on the evil and false."

–Cecil

Questions to Consider:
1. Are you focusing on what is beautiful and good in the world?
2. Did you know that the things you dwell and focus on tend to expand?

My Choice & Commitment:
I choose to   (Circle One)
A. Do nothing about this now.
B. Consider this further.
C. Take Action.

Specific Action Steps I Will Take:
(**Sample Action:** I will write down twelve things that are right with the world and carry it with me in my purse or wallet as a reminder of the good.)

1._____
2._____
3._____

When? (Circle One)
Today   This Week   This Month   Other_____

Fundamental Change

"Fundamental change...involves a qualitative change in our souls as well as a quantitative change in our lives."

–Martin Luther King, Jr.

Questions to Consider:
1. What does this statement mean to you?
2. Can you think of some soul initiatives and practical steps to achieve this great ideal?

My Choice & Commitment:
I choose to   (Circle One)
- A. Do nothing about this now.
- B. Consider this further.
- C. Take Action.

Specific Action Steps I Will Take:
(**Sample Action:** I will mark my calendar to attend a conference by a global empowerment organization to inspire and motivate me toward constructive action options.)

1._____
2._____
3._____

When? (Circle One)
Today   This Week   This Month   Other_____

Week Eight
Celebration of Diversity

Individual and Cultural Differences Enrich Our Life

"Differences can only enrich our experience, and the absence of difference impoverishes us."

–Martha Vancebury and Sylvia W. Silverman

Questions to Consider:
1. Are you able to view differences in others without judgment or bias?
2. How might your life be enriched through making a conscious effort to communicate more with people from other cultures?

My Choice & Commitment:
I choose to   (Circle One)
   A. Do nothing about this now.
   B. Consider this further.
   C. Take Action.

Specific Action Steps I Will Take:
(**Sample Action:** I will attend a community ethnic event and talk with at least three people about their cultural heritage and beliefs.)

1._____
2._____
3._____

When? (Circle One)
   Today   This Week   This Month   Other_____

Honest Differences

"Honest differences are often a healthy sign of progress."

–Mahatma Gandhi

Questions to Consider:
1. Are you open to differences of opinion in discussions with others?
2. What are some ways that honest differences can lead to healthy progress?

My Choice & Commitment:
I choose to   (Circle One)
   A. Do nothing about this now.
   B. Consider this further.
   C. Take Action.

Specific Action Steps I Will Take:
(**Sample Action:** I will form a group with several people who have totally different backgrounds and belief systems. We will agree to discuss our differences openly without judgment.)

1._____
2._____
3._____

When? (Circle One)
   Today   This Week   This Month   Other_____

Language Influences How We View the World

"If we spoke a different language, we would perceive a somewhat different world."

–Ludwig Wittgenstein

Questions to Consider:
1. Did you know that each of us have a somewhat different view of the world according to the culture in which we were born, our language, social conditioning, values and past experiences?
2. Can you allow for the possibility that your view of the world is only one of millions and that your "slice of reality" only represents a tiny portion of the overall picture of reality?

My Choice & Commitment:
I choose to   (Circle One)
   A. Do nothing about this now.
   B. Consider this further.
   C. Take Action.

Specific Action Steps I Will Take:
(**Sample Action:** *Mind Expansion Activity*: Draw a circle that represents the world and divide into as many countries of the world as possible. Inside your country, place a dot and consider the tiny sliver of reality you know.)

1._____
2._____
3._____

When? (Circle One)
   Today   This Week   This Month   Other_____

An Open Mind

"Remember always that your mind must be like a room with many open windows. Let the breeze flow in from all the windows but refuse to be blown away by any one."

–Mohandas Gandhi

Questions to Consider:
1. How open is your mind to different views, lifestyles, and ways of doing things?
2. Can you learn from the diverse range of multi-cultural views without being unduly influenced by charismatic manipulative personalities?

My Choice & Commitment:
I choose to   (Circle One)
   A. Do nothing about this now.
   B. Consider this further.
   C. Take Action.

Specific Action Steps I Will Take:
(**Sample Action:** I will increase my understanding of how our minds become closed to new ideas and ways of doing things by reading an article on "How Prejudices Develop".)

1._____
2._____
3._____

When? (Circle One)
      Today   This Week   This Month   Other_____

Celebrate Differences

"Share our similarities, celebrate our differences."

–M. Scott Peck

Questions to Consider:
1. Do you sometimes see differences in others as a threat?
2. What are some ways we can become more tolerant and less judgmental of those who have different beliefs, lifestyles and appearances? What does it mean to celebrate our differences?

My Choice & Commitment:
I choose to   (Circle One)
    A. Do nothing about this now.
    B. Consider this further.
    C. Take Action.

Specific Action Steps I Will Take:
(**Sample Action:** I will begin consciously practicing cultural relativism, i.e., viewing other cultures' differences through their eyes rather than mine, and avoid the ethnocentrism of judging others according to my own culture's beliefs and practices.)

1._____
2._____
3._____

When? (Circle One)
    Today   This Week   This Month   Other_____

Synergy

"Difference is the beginning of synergy."

–Stephen R. Covey

Questions to Consider:
1. What are some ways in which we can turn differences with others into synergy?
2. How might that positively change our lives?

My Choice & Commitment:
I choose to   (Circle One)
- A. Do nothing about this now.
- B. Consider this further.
- C. Take Action.

Specific Action Steps I Will Take:
(**Sample Action:** I will make a conscious effort to shift my attitude from one of judgment to one of curiosity and possibility when I confront differences in others.)

1._____
2._____
3._____

When? (Circle One)
   Today   This Week   This Month   Other_____

Give Up Prejudices

"It is never too late to give up our prejudices."

–Henry David Thoreau

Questions to Consider:
1. If you gave up one prejudice a week, how long would it take to rid yourself of all prejudices?
2. Why should you make this effort? What would be one positive global outcome if each of us took on this task?

My Choice & Commitment:
I choose to   (Circle One)
A. Do nothing about this now.
B. Consider this further.
C. Take Action.

Specific Action Steps I Will Take:
(**Sample Action:** I will motivate myself to eliminate one prejudice I have about someone whose religious and ethnic background is different from my own by asking them to tell me about their beliefs. I will listen to them with an open, nonjudgmental mind and heart.)

1._____
2._____
3._____

When? (Circle One)
Today   This Week   This Month   Other_____

Week Nine
Peaceful Co-existence

Lasting Peace through Understanding

"Peace cannot be kept by force. It can only be achieved by understanding."

–Albert Einstein

Questions to Consider:
1. Although this important insight has been reiterated in one form or another numerous times by great minds, as well as verified in history's experience, why have we failed to heed it?
2. What are some of the reasons that our understanding lags so far behind our technological advances?

My Choice & Commitment:
I choose to   (Circle One)
   A. Do nothing about this now.
   B. Consider this further.
   C. Take Action.

Specific Action Steps I Will Take:
(**Sample Action:** I will discuss this idea with five other people and generate possible means for influencing those who live by force.)

1._____
2._____
3._____

When? (Circle One)
   Today   This Week   This Month   Other_____

Only Peaceful People Will Have Lasting Peace

"Peace is not a relationship of nations. It is a condition of mind brought about by a serenity of soul. Peace is not merely the absence of war. It is also a state of mind. Lasting peace can come only to peaceful people."

–Jawaharlal Nehru

Questions to Consider:
1. Do you think peace reigns in the heart of most of the people you know?
2. Why do you think this is so?

My Choice & Commitment:
I choose to (Circle One)
A. Do nothing about this now.
B. Consider this further.
C. Take Action.

Specific Action Steps I Will Take:
(**Sample Action:** List six ways in which you can capture and retain a "peace-state-of-mind". Think of it as a commodity over which you have control—*you do*.)

1._____
2._____
3._____

When? (Circle One)
    Today   This Week   This Month   Other_____

As You Give & Live

*"Not as we take, but as we give; not as we pray, but as we live.
These are the things that make for peace, both now and after
Time shall cease."*

–Clarence Urmy

Questions to Consider:
1. Is your life more about taking than giving?
2. Is the way you live making a statement for peace?

My Choice & Commitment:
I choose to   (Circle One)
    A. Do nothing about this now.
    B. Consider this further.
    C. Take Action.

Specific Action Steps I Will Take:
(**Sample Action:** I will demonstrate to an underprivileged person in another country that there are people who care by giving him or her a possession which I cherish, and that will improve their life in some small way.)

1._____
2._____
3._____

When? (Circle One)
    Today   This Week   This Month   Other_____

A Single Nation

"All people are a single nation."

–Qu-ran

Questions to Consider:
1. Are we ready to believe this great truth?
2. If this were etched in our hearts, how would it impact our treatment of "other" nations? Will we ever rise above the schism of "them and us"?

My Choice & Commitment:
I choose to   (Circle One)
A. Do nothing about this now.
B. Consider this further.
C. Take Action.

Specific Action Steps I Will Take:
(**Sample Action:** I will write down five of the common and unifying characteristics of human beings around the globe to help me affirm and live this great truth.)

1._____
2._____
3._____

When? (Circle One)
    Today   This Week   This Month   Other_____

Peace Is Up to the People

"I like to believe that people in the long run are going to do more to promote peace than our governments. Indeed, I think that people want peace so much that one of these days governments had better get out of the way and let them have it."

Dwight D. Eisenhower

Questions to Consider:
1. Do you believe that you have a role to play in international peaceful co-existence?
2. How would you define your role here?

My Choice & Commitment:
I choose to   (Circle One)
- A. Do nothing about this now.
- B. Consider this further.
- C. Take Action.

Specific Action Steps I Will Take:
(**Sample Action:** I will let my government know how I feel about acts of war by regularly writing or Emailing my government officials.)

1._____
2._____
3._____

When? (Circle One)
    Today   This Week   This Month   Other_____

Coexistence

"It's coexistence or no existence."

–Bertrand Russell

Questions to Consider:
1. Do you believe it's possible to coexist with other nations in a way that lets us solve our differences through nonviolent means?
2. What are some of the ways that we can move in this direction?

My Choice & Commitment:
I choose to   (Circle One)
   A. Do nothing about this now.
   B. Consider this further.
   C. Take Action.

Specific Action Steps I Will Take:
(**Sample Action:** I will read a work by Mohandas Gandhi on nonviolence to educate myself on the application of nonviolence principles.)

1._____
2._____
3._____

When? (Circle One)
   Today   This Week   This Month   Other_____

Begin at Home

"If we want to create a world without violence, we must begin at home. Government decrees or compassionate legislation are meaningless unless the values they espouse are practiced in the family."

–Alvin F. Poussaint

Questions to Consider:
1. What values do you practice in your home or school?
2. Are we teaching our children to resolve conflicts peacefully?

My Choice & Commitment:
I choose to   (Circle One)
   A. Do nothing about this now.
   B. Consider this further.
   C. Take Action.

Specific Action Steps I Will Take:
(**Sample Action:** I will help counteract the massive effects on our children of violence in television, video games, and movies by living out the values of compassion and kindness in my own home.)

1._____
2._____
3._____

When? (Circle One)
   Today   This Week   This Month   Other_____

Week Ten
You Make the Difference

Positive Global Change Begins with the Individual

"Think about the kind of world you want to live and work in. What do you need to know to build that world?..."

–Kropotkin

Questions to Consider:
1. What is your vision of an ideal world?
2. What knowledge, skills and actions will help to create that world?

My Choice & Commitment:
I choose to   (Circle One)
A. Do nothing about this now.
B. Consider this further.
C. Take Action.

Specific Action Steps I Will Take:
(**Sample Action:** I will write a one page draft of my vision for an ideal world, and the knowledge and skills I have to help build that world.)

1._____
2._____
3._____

When? (Circle One)
Today   This Week   This Month   Other_____

Give Your Best

"...give to the world the best you have, and the best will come back to you."

–Madeline Bridges

Questions to Consider:
1. Are you motivated to give your personal best to the world?
2. Can you believe that when you give your best, it will come back to you?

My Choice & Commitment:
I choose to   (Circle One)
A. Do nothing about this now.
B. Consider this further.
C. Take Action.

Specific Action Steps I Will Take:
(**Sample Action:** Take five minutes to ponder the following statement: "When I give my heartfelt best to the task at hand, I do not need to concern myself with the outcome. It will take care of itself.")

1._____
2._____
3._____

When? (Circle One)
Today   This Week   This Month   Other_____

The Realm of Possibility

"I cannot discover that anyone knows enough to say definitely what is and what is not possible."

–Henry Ford

Questions to Consider:
1. Do you avoid trying to tackle some of the big problems of the world because you believe them to be impossible tasks?
2. Do you believe they are the responsibility of someone else, not you?

My Choice & Commitment:
I choose to   (Circle One)
- A. Do nothing about this now.
- B. Consider this further.
- C. Take Action.

Specific Action Steps I Will Take:
(**Sample Action:** I will begin "acting as if" I am the person responsible for solving an "impossible" world problem.)

1._____
2._____
3._____

When? (Circle One)
   Today   This Week   This Month   Other_____

Do Something Remarkable

"Expose yourself to the possibility of doing something remarkable."

–C. Cunningham

Questions to Consider:
1. Have you ever considered that you could do something remarkable?
2. Are you willing to take that leap? What have you got to lose?

My Choice & Commitment:
I choose to   (Circle One)
   A. Do nothing about this now.
   B. Consider this further.
   C. Take Action.

Specific Action Steps I Will Take:
(**Sample Action:** Write a one paragraph description of the most remarkable thing I could do to improve global communication and understanding.)

1._____
2._____
3._____

When? (Circle One)
   Today   This Week   This Month   Other_____

An Individual Project

*"Western thought has programmed the individual to believe
that the extrapolation of the laws and principles of our universe
is the function of science and government, and that this is not a
project for the individual. However, it is the individual who
delivers the mail, not the post office."*

–Rabbi Philip S. Berg

Questions to Consider:
1. Do you believe that the weighty problems of life should
   be left up to the government or someone else to solve?
2. What are three specific individual actions you can take
   this week to improve global understanding?

My Choice & Commitment:
I choose to   (Circle One)
   A. Do nothing about this now.
   B. Consider this further.
   C. Take Action.

Specific Action Steps I Will Take:
(**Sample Action:** I will block out time to research and come to
a better understanding of another country and their practices.
Next I will Email a person in that country the things I
appreciate and admire most about their culture.)

1._____
2._____
3._____

When? (Circle One)
     Today   This Week   This Month   Other_____

Win a Victory for Humanity

"Be ashamed to die until you have won some victory for humanity."

–Horace Mann

Questions to Consider:
1. What victory can you win for humanity?
2. Will you rise up to that possibility within yourself or die ashamed?

My Choice & Commitment:
I choose to   (Circle One)
   A. Do nothing about this now.
   B. Consider this further.
   C. Take Action.

Specific Action Steps I Will Take:
(**Sample Action:** I will mindstorm about all the possible victories I might win for humanity and then act on one of them.)

1._____
2._____
3._____

When? (Circle One)
   Today   This Week   This Month   Other_____

You Change the World Everyday

"Everyday you change the world. Today will be no exception."

–Ralph Marston

Questions to Consider:
1. How did the world change today because of you?
2. How will it change tomorrow and the next day and the next day because of you?

My Choice & Commitment:
I choose to   (Circle One)
A. Do nothing about this now.
B. Consider this further.
C. Take Action.

Specific Action Steps I Will Take:
(**Sample Action:** List three ways the world changed today because of you. List three ways you'd like it to change in the next year because of you.)

1._____
2._____
3._____

When? (Circle One)
Today   This Week   This Month   Other_____

Actions for Global Understanding
75 Actions You Can Start Taking Today!

Listed below are a variety of actions you can take to influence the course of global understanding. You are probably already acting on several of these. Use them as a springboard for your own ideas, to adapt to your unique personality, situation and circumstances. I recommend you place a checkmark by those that resonate with you. Then, mark at least one in your planning calendar each month to follow through on.

1. Join a Global Online Forum with like-minded people to discuss human rights issues. Help promote dialogue and international cooperation. Go to Mandat International for a calendar of international meetings, online forums, and 100's of useful links. www.mandint.org

2. Become a "global partner" for a community of women in a third world country in need of support. (See www.soroptimist.org international programs.)

3. Use the $25.00 a month that you're spending on snacks or cigarettes to sponsor a child in another country so they will have access to clean water, food, and health care. (See www.childreach.org)

4. Organize a "White Ribbon Campaign" in your community to help end domestic violence. See www.whiteribbon.com.

5. Have a "Global Awareness" home party and ask everyone to bring one idea to discuss.

6. Join or form a group in your area to discuss a global issue of interest such as sex trafficking, poverty and

nonviolence. Check out your local Community College for information and handouts to provide to members.

7. Use art as a tool to increase global understanding. (Visit http://lov-e.com/Global_8.html and click on the "Art for the World" link.) This site also lists dozens of other websites you'll want to explore.

8. Volunteer two hours a week in a community organization that is working toward the solution of global issues.

9. Send an Email to your government officials on an injustice you have observed. (See http://www.e-thepeople.org/ for Email addresses of senators and representatives in your location, along with forms and other information.)

10. Work with a local organization in your community to raise funds for disaster relief in another country. Be a volunteer or make a direct donation to www.doctorswithoutborders.org

11. Join or form a book club whose books include global issues and celebrate the interconnectedness of life. (Check out Adelante Book of the Month Club, Oprah's Book Club or Heartsong Books at www.heartsongbooks.com.) Inspirational messages are also available on this website.

12. Plan an ethnic potluck dinner with people from different ethnic groups in your community. It needn't be elaborate. Ask each to bring their favorite dish.

13. Click on this website to provide one cup of food to feed the hungry: www.thehungersite.com (free, paid for by sponsor banner advertising). Build global understanding by helping those in need. Send an

eCard from this site to help combat hunger and cultivate peace.

14. Read one article or book a month on a different culture. Check with your library for suggestions, then choose according to your interests.

15. Set aside the two hours a week you used to spend watching television on researching a world problem such as poverty or global warming.

16. In lieu of a vacation, volunteer a week or two of your time in another country for teaching basic skills such as sewing, knitting or dressmaking to someone in need. (See www.ifuw.com for a list of some organizations that coordinate volunteer activities.) Also see Global Exchange at http://www.globalexchange.org.

17. Obtain a DVD documentary on another culture to learn more about their lifestyle and practices. A variety of these can be found online for a nominal fee or free.

18. Take a class on foreign affairs at your local community college or at an online university. Or join one of the Great Decisions discussion groups. See Foreign Policy Association at www.fpa.org for a group near you.

19. Promote intercultural understanding on your next vacation to another country, by visiting or staying with locals and sharing information. See The Hospitality Club www.hospitalityclub.com where you can post messages and meet people from dozens of different countries.

20. Volunteer to give a talk to a class at a local grade school or high school about a culture that you're

familiar with. This can be a very rewarding experience.

21. Support a survivor of war in another country. (See www.womenforwomen.org for sponsorship information.)

22. Talk to a teacher or principal at a local school about including global issues in their curriculum.

23. Donate funds through an organization to purchase sewing and knitting machines in a third world country. (E.g., see www.virginiagildersleeve.net)

24. Hold a bake sale or garage sale and donate the proceeds to an organization involved in working toward the resolution of global issues.

25. Set up a booth exhibit at a community trade show to promote "Global Understanding".

26. Mindstorm for one hour this week, listing fifteen possible means for increasing global understanding. Then follow through on one of them.

27. Regularly read a foreign newspaper on the internet to get a different point of view. (If you have a relatively new computer and software it can be translated into English.) Simply enter the name of a country and "newspaper" in your favorite search engine.

28. Get together with a group of colleagues or friends and mindstorm on various ways to raise funds to help finance a specific global project.

29. Volunteer two weeks of your time in a third world country for literacy training. (See www.ifuw.com or www.globalexchange.org for organizations that coordinate training classes in different countries.)

30. Celebrate cultural diversity in your home. Check out the books, music, crafts and artwork in your house. What kind of statement does your home make about you and your values?

31. Give a gift of crayons and a writing tablet to a child in another country. E.g., this could be through contacts you have in your church, school or a local organization.

32. Donate a book you've read, DVD or music that increases global awareness and understanding to someone in another country.

33. "Travel with a Cause" on your next vacation. Check out MiraMed International's Russia Cruises. Personally deliver clothing, medicine and supplies to Russian orphanages on your cruise. (See http://www.miramed.com.) Have fun and help others.

34. Volunteer to teach a group in another country a skill you possess (E.g., computer or communication skills; parenting practices; basic bookkeeping; starting a business).

35. If you have a web site, show your support of human rights by adding a human rights banner to your site. (E.g., see Human Rights Watch at http://www.hrw.org/banner/.) If you don't have a web site, suggest that local businesses post a human rights banner.

36. Train a group of trainers to assist others in basic skills that will also promote intercultural goodwill and cooperation.

37. Establish contact with someone from another ethnic group than your country of origin and invite them to join you for coffee or lunch. How? Meet new people

at a local ethnic festival or strike up a conversation with merchants where you shop.

38. Attend art exhibits sponsored by different ethnic groups. Ask questions, learn and share.

39. Join an online forum on global issues. Share your insights and listen to others to learn and better understand their point of view. Make power accountable. (Check out www.commoncause.org/causenet.)

40. Set aside two hours to research some of the inhuman policies and practices occurring in different countries. Send a letter to your government officials. Start by visiting United Nations Human Rights at http://www.un.org/rights for fact sheets on injustices taking place around the globe.

41. Volunteer to work in another country through one of the many organizations acting to make a difference. Some organizations will pay your travel expenses and other basic costs. Try International Executive Service Corps (IESC) of Stamford, Connecticut, USA. www.iesc.org

42. Shop stores, catalogs and online to earn rebates for the causes and organizations you support at Schoolpop. See www.Schoolpop.com.

43. Sponsor or organize an arts and crafts exhibit in your area with products from twelve third world countries.

44. Travel with a purpose by visiting one of the humanitarian project sites in another country. (E.g., visit Heifer International to learn more about their caring gifts to end world hunger www.heifer.org)

45. Give an individual in another country the means to help themselves with a micro-loan to start her own business. See http://www.katalysis.org

46. Begin corresponding with women in other parts of the world on a topic of interest through a web listserv. See International Federation of University Women for listservs on different topics such as health, education and women's issues at http://www.ifuw.org.

47. Shop in an ethnic region of your city and ask shop owners about their families in other countries.

48. Through "Adopt a Village" (AAV), you can help a struggling Mayan family to own and farm their own land. With your support a family of migrant laborers working on coffee fields for less than subsistence wages can hope to achieve a healthy, productive life. See http://www.az.com/~rhicks/help.html for information.

49. Draft a well-thought out letter on some aspect of a social injustice and Email it to twelve online newspapers or journals.

50. Write a personal note of encouragement to a woman in a war torn country. Contact humanitarian groups working in the country or embassies for information.

51. Make arrangements with local officials to set up a table in a shopping mall with flyers on Global Understanding.

52. Invite a group of friends over and have each give a five to ten minute demonstration on some aspect of a country in which they've traveled or researched.

53. Build cooperation and compassion in children by encouraging games, toys and activities that celebrate

cultural diversity and nonviolence. Avoid buying guns and games that breed hate and violence.

54. Influence writers of family and children's television shows to have more value-driven characters who take a stand against social injustices. Contact them by Email and through the news media.

55. Charge purchases to a credit card obtained from a humanitarian organization that receives a percentage of the sale at no cost to you. Visit Amnesty at www.amnestyusa.org/visa.

56. Attend a meeting of an ethnic organization in your community that is open to guests.

57. Spend one month or more as a human rights intern in Russia (Russian language skills not required.) See http://www.miramedinstitute.org for information.

58. Distribute brochures at your local club, school or church on one of the global humanitarian organizations you support.

59. Give a value gift in honor of a friend or family's birthday, anniversary or religious holiday. Visit Alternative Gifts International www.altgifts.org to learn about gifts that empower people and promote global goodwill.

60. Host an "Information Session" in your home on a global organization making a difference. Email or write the organization for free materials to hand out.

61. Ask your employer to match contributions to a humanitarian organization that you support.

62. Expand your mind by listening to interviews by noted scientists and humanitarians on an educational world

broadcasting network. Visit New Dimensions World Broadcasting Network at www.newdimensions.org.

63. Boycott products produced by corporations who violate fair trade practices and human rights. See www.business-ethics.com.

64. Take part in a community activity such as a rally or signature-gathering drive that supports a global issue of concern.

65. Add your voice to others protesting violations of human rights by joining a Mailing List of a global organization. See www.moveon.org.

66. Stay informed by subscribing to free Email reports of an organization that keeps you current on human rights news around the world (E.g., see Human Rights Watch at http://www.hrw.org/act/subscribe-mlists/subscribe.htm.)

67. Donate a portion of the money you spend on online consumer purchases to a charity of choice by setting up a "charity shopping portal". It only takes a few minutes and it's free! Visit this website to set up an account: www.iGive.com. After joining, tell your friends and get $1.00 for your cause every time you refer a new shopper.

68. Recycle used printer cartridges, cell phones and other items to earn cash for your school or organization. http://www.schoolpop.com/cgi/myschool.cgi?pid=3.

69. Respond to media articles that present cultural misinformation, partial information or biased views. Let the public know the other side. If not you, who?

70. Adopt-A-Goat in Guatemala. A goat can provide a cup of milk each day for a Mayan child and help

prevent malnutrition and diseases relating to lack of nutrition. (See http://www.az.com/~rhicks/help.html for information. You will receive a photograph of your goat and may choose her name.)

71. Be a "Virtual Volunteer". Many online humanitarian organizations and charities need help with Email correspondence, graphics, programming, research and writing. See www.NetAid.org for a worldwide directory of virtual volunteering positions.

72. Purchase products from an organization where the proceeds go to support a cause you believe in. See Amnesty International www.amnestyusa.org/store.

73. Refuse to support businesses and organizations that continue to test their products on animals. Visit People for the Ethical Treatment of Animals (PETA) www.peta.org and www.caringconsumer.com.

74. Put your dollars where your principles are by investing in socially screened mutual funds. Typical screens include weapons, tobacco, fair hiring polices and products that enhance the quality of life. Check out Capital Missions Company http://www.capitalmissions.com/social/index.html for a list of social investment providers.

75. Set your clock radio, iPod or computer to wake up to inspirational music rather than the alarm and start your day on a happier note. Remember your attitude has an impact on all those you communicate with during the day.

Inspiration & Insight Without Action Won't Change Anything

If Not Now, When?

A Personal Thank You from Jan Gault

Thank you for reading this book. I value your input and would love to hear from you. I invite you to Email me at my personal Email Address: drjan1@earthlink.net. Let me know three actions you are taking to increase global understanding and the approximate date they were initiated.

Please read the **Global Person Pledge** on the next page and if it resonates with you, sign, tear out and Email or snail mail to me. You can also print it from my website at www.drjan.net/globalperson.

Sign up for a Free Subscription to my online Newsletter (Ezine) at www.drjan.net/betterworld to receive bimonthly announcements about Free Inspirational Podcast Messages, Teleconferences, Special Events, Product Discounts & Offers, New Books & Tapes, Free Excerpts, and more!

As a Global Person I pledge to...

- Be proactive and stay informed about the ways in which my daily activities can make a difference in lives around the world.

- Begin with myself; knowing that only by taking care of my own mental, emotional, spiritual and physical health can I be an effective agent of change. Only then can I set a good example for others.

- Serve my community in ways that benefit all.

- Keep an open mind to ideological differences and practices, searching for common ground and possibilities for cooperation.

- Appreciate and learn from differences. I will strive to be nonjudgmental and accepting, looking for the best in others and resolving any conflicts that arise through nonviolent means.

- Strive to hold a sustainable vision of world prosperity, universal education, socio-economic justice and peace.

"What you hold in your thoughts is what you bring into the world."
~High Star

_____
Signed by

_____
Date

AUTHOR PROFILE

Jan L. Gault, Ph.D. is a social psychologist, university instructor, creative time specialist, and the author of many articles and books including **Free Time—Making Your Leisure Count** (Wiley & Sons) and **The Mighty Power of your Beliefs**...Dream, Believe, Prosper!

Dr. Jan has taught at a number of universities including University of Hawaii, University of Phoenix, Central Texas College, and has devoted over fifteen years educating and empowering people to live a richer, more rewarding life. She was co-founder and president of Opportunity Network West, Inc., a San Francisco based entrepreneurial association. Her programs have been presented in universities and through a variety of business and professional organizations worldwide. Jan has been featured on over 200 radio/television networks and media throughout the United States and Canada. Her articles, books excerpts and reviews have been published in *Glamour Magazine, San Francisco Business Journal, Bottom Line Personal, Christian Science Monitor* and the *Fedco Reporter* among others.

Jan lives in Hawaii where she teaches university classes in psychology and has a private practice specializing in personal-global empowerment and better living.

Order Additional Copies of this Book & Other Products by Jan Gault

Order additional copies of this book for your family and friends. It makes a great gift! Go to www.amazon.com to place your order online or pick up a copy at your local bookstore. Amazon.com is currently offering a 30% discount on Jan's *The Mighty Power of Your Beliefs – Dream, Believe, Prosper.*

Download or stream Jan's inspirational podcast messages at www.drjan.net/quotes. Click on the audio icon to listen.

Be sure and visit Dr. Jan's Personal-Global Empowerment Shop of unique gift products
http://www.cafepress.com/GlobalGood

For information on training programs & consultations, please contact

Jan Gault International©
P.O. Box 75315
Eaton Square
Honolulu, Hawaii 96836
Tel 808-593-3648 Fax 800-851-6114
Email: uptime@drjan.net
Web site: http://www.drjan.net/betterworld

www.ingramcontent.com/pod-product-compliance
Lightning Source LLC
Chambersburg PA
CBHW031212270326
41931CB00006B/530